The Dragon Lady's HANDBOOK

Fran Moeller Gatins

The Dragon Lady's

H
A
N
D
B
O
O
K

Chapter & Verse, Ink

Copyright© 2000 by Frances Moeller Gatins

All rights reserved,
including the publication in whole or in part in any form.

Published in the United States of America by Chapter & Verse, Ink

Library of Congress Catalog

ISBN: 0-9676955-1-1

Manufactured in the United States of America

Designed by Douglas Steel
Editorial support by Carol McKenna

For Joe and Demian

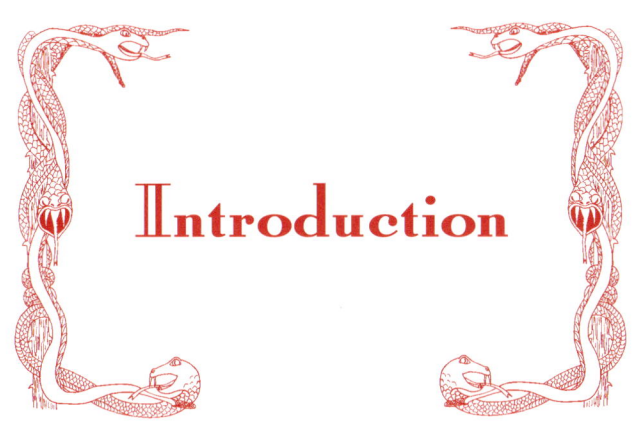

Introduction

The Dragon is one of mankind's oldest symbols, and a remarkably universal one. In cultures around the world, it has been a source of veneration, fear and fascination.

The Western Dragon

While the earliest descriptions of Dragons seem to have come from the Sumerians, in the West Dragon iconography developed to its fullest in the Middle Ages.

Medieval artists pictured the Dragon as incorporating elements of many creatures. It had an eagle's throat and legs, representative of heavenly or cosmic possibilities; a serpent's body, indicating knowledge that is hidden within the Earth; a bat's wings, symbolizing the intellect's ability to soar; and the lion's tail (Leo in Western astrology) with the arrow twisting back on itself (Scorpio), indicating emotion and intuition.

This iconography demonstrates that Dragons encompass three levels of being: the cosmic or spiritual, the perceptual or sensory and the earthy. Consequently, Dragons are believed to be intermediaries between heaven and earth. Christian symbolism focused on the "earthy" part of this equation, "earthy" being interpreted as base.

Dragons were depicted as an evil to be conquered, both in the world and within the person. Medieval knights embarked on quests to find and slay Dragons, and the image of a Dragon chained or underfoot came to represent God triumphant over Satan.

On the other hand, another familiar Western icon is the very positive Ouroboros. This circular image of a Dragon or serpent swallowing its tail represents cyclic processes, especially time. Association with the continuous, rhythmic cycle of nature is attributed to Dragons all over the world.

The Chinese Dragon

In Chinese iconography, the Dragon is omnipresent and nearly always benevolent, although it can be very destructive at times. The Chinese Dragon or *lung* is associated with water in all its forms, and therefore with life itself. It is often depicted with images of clouds, waterspouts, lakes, pools, ponds, storms and lightning. In the spring, Dragons ascend to the heavens to stimulate rain. In the fall, they descend into the earthly waters.

As in the West, Dragons are intermediaries and travel freely through the "above" and the "below." They are venerated as bearers of blessings and considered first among all animals that swim or crawl.

In spite of what Westerners would consider negative qualities, the Chinese Dragon is thought of as virtuous—the epitome of goodness, might and vigor. That it sometimes brings tornadoes and hurricanes, scorches with its fiery breath and occasionally devours people is considered small cost for its presence.

Overall, the Dragon brings happiness and blessings to humans, yet it is ready to strike down anyone who offends the gods. By extension, it is a symbol of the emperor. He, too, was expected to be an intermediary between the gods and humans, heaven and earth.

A much older and more ubiquitous icon than its Western counterpart, the Chinese Dragon embodies diverse qualities and incorporates some surprising creatures within its form. The camel, deer, rabbit, fish, cow, frog, tiger and hawk have all been part of the Chinese Dragon at one time or another.

Because Dragons travel freely between worlds, because they are associated with water, and incorporate many creatures within their bodies, their world is one of continual flux and change. Adaptability and flexibility are characteristics of Dragons—and highly desirable qualities for Dragon Ladies. Other qualities are a love of music and literature and supernatural strength. On the not-so-positive side are ferocity, litigiousness, gluttony and a propensity to rest frequently.

The Dragon Lady

The Dragon is one of the 12 animals of Chinese lunar astrology, and if you were born in a Year of the Dragon, you are a bona fide Dragon Lady. Because the Chinese and Western New Years begin at different times, you must check the astrological chart to determine if you belong to this select group.

In Chinese astrology, each year is influenced by one of the Five Elements: Wood, Fire, Earth, Metal and Water. While Chinese astrology is as complicated as Western, your animal sign and the element that influences it are primary indicators of your personality and character.

Dragon Years and Their Element

1916—17	Fire
1928—29	Earth
1940—41	Metal
1952—53	Water
1964—65	Wood
1976—77	Fire
1988—89	Earth
2000—01	Metal
2012—13	Water

Chinese and Western years don't coincide exactly.
To see if your birthday falls precisely within a Dragon Year,
please look on the last page.

The Five Elements

Wood is related to intuition. A healthy Wood person will be expansive, progressive and flexible, trusting her inner guidance to lead her easily into the new. Wood people need to feel useful and are prone to overwork. Expanding too far and fast, going out on a limb and feeling overwhelmed are signs of too much Wood; timidity, feeling powerless and "staying small," of too little.

Archetype:
The tree, grounded in the earth and reaching ever upward.

Color: *Green, sometimes blue*

Fire relates to emotions which, when healthy, foster positive relationships. A healthy Fire type is dynamic, compassionate, assertive and creative. Fire people are great communicators but can get over-stimulated and "flame out." Other signs of excess Fire are impatience and aggression. The proverbial "cold fish" has too little Fire and probably not much energy.

Archetype:
The flame, burning steadily.

Color: *Red*

Earth relates to the physical. Healthy Earth people are grounded in the moment, sensual, organized and practical. They value harmony and loyalty and are peacemakers but they can get stuck in details, family and

people-pleasing. Being conservative, unspontaneous and anal retentive indicate too much of the Earth element, while being a "space cadet" indicates too little.

Archetype:
Earth herself, healthy, productive and beautiful
Color: *Yellow*

Metal relates to mental activity. Golden Dragon Ladies are Metal people—quick-witted, physically strong and determined. They seek mastery and order but can end up rigid perfectionists. A sharp tongue and thinking "inside the box" are signs of too much Metal; indecisiveness and muddled thinking of too little.

Archetype:
The gemstone, enduring and brilliant.
Color: *White*

Water relates to spirituality. Water people are relaxed, flowing, mystical and mysterious. But their gift of imagination can mutate into telling tall tales, a desire for truth into hoarding secrets. Too much Water shows up as passivity and inconstancy; too little, anxiety and an inability to handle stress.

Archetype:
Bodies of water.
Color: *Black*

Are You A Dragon Lady?

Because the Dragon incorporates
so many animals within itself,
you may well contain Dragon-Lady qualities.
If you do, you will recognize
yourself in this Handbook.

Dragons are ancient

and nearly universal creatures,

therefore you will be recognized

wherever you go.

Dress accordingly.

Treat yourself as

a mythic, magical, exotic being

and you won't be nonplussed

when others do.

Always keep your scales polished.

You never know who's watching.

Boredom is a very unhealthy state

for Dragon Ladies.

One way to forestall it:

always have at least

three projects going at the same time.

Learn to delight in change, because that is the basic condition of the Dragon Lady's world.

For a Dragon Lady, accumulated knowledge is less valuable than now-knowing. Practice being fully present to the moment.

Keep your body as supple as your mind. Do some snaky dancing regularly.

Dragon Ladies

expect to be

listened to

respectfully,

so make sure

your brain and your mouth

are working together

harmoniously.

Dragons are considered eccentric by many people. This is ridiculous. Pay no attention.

Expect to be misunderstood.

"Vigilance personified" is often a description of Dragons. Know the difference between vigilance and paranoia.

Your power can attract people who want to be dependent on you. Don't allow it.

A Dragon Lady's mouth

is a mighty weapon.

Use only as much fire as necessary.

It's okay to blow smoke

to deflect a conversation

from subjects you

don't want to discuss.

There is no such thing as an average Dragon Lady.

A Dragon Lady's tail

is as powerful as her mouth.

Learn how and when to use it,

and regularly exercise your tail muscles

so that you can control them.

Dragon Ladies are at home

on and in all the elements

(Earth, Wood, Metal, Water, Fire),

therefore facility in many areas

is within your power.

Cultivate as many of your gifts

as you can without exhausting yourself.

Fatigue makes Dragon Ladies cranky and snappish. Get enough rest.

Pouting and sulking are exceedingly unbecoming to Dragon Ladies, probably because Dragon Ladies are rarely "cute." Avoid this behavior altogether.

Dragon Ladies

function best when

working on a project.

It is best if the

project is not human.

Certain Dragon Ladies

are known for volubility,

even braggadocio.

Value silence.

Accept that the basic Dragon nature is solitary. Release any expectation that someone or something outside yourself can bring you happiness.

Dragons sparkle most

when open and generous.

Share yourself

and your resources.

If you are a Dragon who likes to fly frequently, be sure you have adequate grounding time. This is especially important for Golden Dragons. Earth Dragons, on the other hand, should make a point of getting off the ground at least once a week.

If you're going to fly,

make sure your wings

are strong enough

to support you,

and that you have

a big enough place

for takeoff and landing.

A support team

doesn't hurt either.

The exotic Dragon Lady can feel "other," and isolate herself from normal human contact. You don't have to become a social Dragonfly, but do make an effort to get out of your lair regularly.

Despite great native vitality, Dragons are not immune to physical problems. Know what your body likes best and be lavish with it.

Dragon gifts

can also lead into

the weeds of arrogance.

Self-confidence

is a great fertilizer,

but arrogance

is choking.

Because the Dragon

has power,

you do not need to use it.

Be magnanimous

and kind

in your dealings with humans.

If you have a little Dragonette,

encourage her to develop her gifts,

not her ego.

Be sure you are a star in your life.

Supporting roles are only

to be played in the lives of others.

Spread your wings,

on any or all levels

(physical, spiritual, scientific, artistic,

intellectual, emotional, etc.)

at least once a day.

You may elect not to fly,

but you'll still want

all your parts in good working order.

A Dragon Lady's perceptions can seem like so much hot air to the unevolved. Know what you can talk about with whom.

Seek the company of other Dragon Ladies from time to time. At least you won't have to explain yourself.

Dragons incorporate elements of dangerous and aggressive animals. This confers a certain "natural authority" that can inspire both fear and envy. Know if and how you want to use this.

The exceptionally keen eyesight
of Dragons often extends to the
gifts of wisdom and prophecy.
Do not appear surprised when people
think you know more than you actually do.
Cultivate a secretive smile
and an air of mystery.

Be comfortable with power, since yours will attract people whether or not you consciously want it to.

A Dragon Lady's world is one of continual change and becoming. Accept that this is part of your nature and your path, and it will be less frightening and frustrating.

No mission, goal or project you take on will satisfy you indefinitely. Immerse yourself fully in whatever you are doing and you will not suspect yourself of flightiness or flakiness when your Inner Self tells you to move on.

People are aware of Dragon Ladies whether or not you're aware of them. Since camouflage is difficult, try to be your gracious and graceful self at all times with all people.

Dragons can be selfish

and have a cheap streak as well.

Practice generosity,

with others and yourself.

In the Dragon world,

a basic principle is that everything

is connected to everything else

and is constantly changing.

Be fluid.

No other being

can fully satisfy a Dragon.

Cultivate your Higher Self

and your Higher Power.

It's okay to crash

and burn occasionally,

in fact you

should expect to.

Just don't do it

too publicly too often.

If you encounter a
Dragon Lady sleeping, let her lie.
She is probably digesting one of
her life's many changes.

Acknowledgments

My knowledge of Dragons was enhanced by the following books: *A Dictionary of Symbols* by J. E. Cirlot; *Dictionary of Subjects & Symbols in Art* by James Hall; *Chinese Animal Symbolisms* by Ong Hean-Tatt; and *The New Astrology* by Suzanne White.

I am indebted to Chungliang "Al" Huang, TaiJi teacher extraordinaire, for my basic understanding of things Chinese, especially the Five Elements; to QiGong master Ken Cohen, and to Terah Kathryn Collins of the Western School of Feng Shui for expanding that understanding.

To all the Dragon Ladies in my life, official and unofficial, I send my profound thanks. You know why, and you know who you are.

Dragon Years and Their Corresponding Western Dates

February 3, 1916–January 22, 1917. January 23, 1928–February 9, 1929.
February 8, 1940–January 26, 1941. January 27, 1952–February 13, 1953.
February 13, 1964–February 1, 1965. January 31, 1976–February 17, 1977.
February 17, 1988–February 5, 1989. February 5, 2000–January 23, 2001.

To Order The Dragon Lady's Handbook

Call 1-888-285-8486, e-mail ChapVerseInk@aol.com,
or write to:
Chapter & Verse, Ink,
224 East 18th St., Suite 3A, NY, NY 10003.